# DISCOVER THE BLUES

## WRITTEN & ILLUSTRATED BY SAM JIMENEZ

Published by

musicopedia™

Discover the Blues
by Sam Jimenez

Musicopedia Media
musicopediamedia@gmail.com

First publication in The United States by Musicopedia Media.

All text, illustrations, and content
©2025 Sam Jimenez ALL RIGHTS RESERVED

Library of Congress Cataloging-in-Publication data is available.

Paperback ISBN: 979-8-218-74616-2

This book is dedicated to the memory of
**Greg "Slim Lively" Johnson**
Or as I called him,
**Greg "The Real King of the Blues" Johnson**

Whether he was serving as the Cascade Blues Association's President in his hometown of Portland, OR, or helping things run smoothly for the Blues Foundation in Memphis, TN, Greg was all-in—100%. I've never known anyone more dedicated to supporting the blues and blues musicians. He was a true superhero and a great friend to so many of us. We miss you, Greg!

# CONTENTS

What Is The Blues? ................................. 1

1   What Makes The Blues, "The Blues?" ............ 7

2   The Source of the Blues ...................... 21

3   The Weirdest Music Ever Heard ............... 29

4   A Quiet Beginning ........................... 37

5   And Then Things Got Loud! .................. 61

6   The Blues Expands Its Audience ............. 77

7   The Blues Goes To Hollywood ............... 97

8   The Most Important Era For The Blues ....... 109

    References & Further Reading ............... 129

**Wow—what a question!**

According to Wikipedia, "Blues is a music genre and musical form which originated in the Deep South of the United States around the 1870s by African Americans, from roots in African musical traditions, African-American work songs, and spirituals."

Okay... they're not wrong.

But *YAWN*. The blues is so much more than that. The blues is a *feeling!*

Sometimes the feeling is good, sometimes the feeling is bad—but it always makes you feel *alive*. And alive is the most important feeling there is, *right?*

The history of the blues is full of emotions: pain, joy, heartbreak, loneliness, happiness, anger, fear, grief—every kind of feeling you can imagine.

The phrase "the blues" probably comes from an older expression: *the blue devils.* That used to mean the scary, sad feelings people got when they were sick or going through something tough— like hallucinations from alcohol withdrawal. Later, it just meant feeling down or depressed.

Because of that, some folks think the blues is just sad music. Or that listening to it will make you feel worse. But that's not true! In fact, listening to the blues when you're feeling low can actually help lift you back up.

Back in the day, some people even called the blues "The Devil's Music."

There were wild stories about musicians selling their souls to the Devil in exchange for amazing guitar skills. The legend said if you went to the crossroads at midnight and handed your guitar to the Devil, he'd re-tune it, give it back, and *BAM—*

you'd become a blues master. But now you owed him your soul.

Cool story... but total superstition.

The real way those musicians got so good? They practiced their butts off!

The blues has always been a way of telling stories through music.

And those stories? They weren't always sad.

Sure, the blues was born out of hard times, so a lot of early songs were about pain, loss, or trouble. But there are *plenty* of blues songs about love, laughter, dancing, friendship—even food.

That's the magic of the blues: whatever the feeling is, it's real. And that makes it powerful.

These days, blues isn't just about lyrics or subject matter. It's a *sound*. A *groove*. A *vibe*.

When you hear just a few notes, you know—it's the blues.

A lot of people discover the blues by hearing it in a movie or TV show. It grabs their ears, stops them in their tracks, and makes them say, "Whoa. What is *this* music?"

Some musicians hear the blues once—and that's it. They're hooked. They never want to play anything else again. That's how powerful it is!

In fact, the blues has influenced almost every genre of popular music—from rock and roll, to hip hop, to pop.

So, what is the blues? That's easy. The blues is one of the most powerful forms of expression ever created.

This book is a short introduction to the blues—where it came from, who helped shape it, and why it still matters.

In the pages ahead, you'll meet some unforgettable musicians, hear wild stories from the early days, learn where the blues came from, and see how it shaped music all over the world. Hopefully, it gives you a lifelong passion for learning about the blues—and more importantly, listening to it.

And maybe, just maybe, it'll inspire you to carry it forward and pass it on, too.

Because so much of the music you listen to today started out as the blues—long, long ago...

# WHAT MAKES THE BLUES, "THE BLUES?"

The differences between musical styles—called *genres*—can be subtle. It might be the instruments, the way the songs are sung or played, the rhythm, or even just the feeling. Every genre has its own recipe—and the blues is no exception.

Before we dive into the wild history and unforgettable people who made the blues what it is, let's break down what gives it its sound, style, and soul.

In this section, we're going to explore the ingredients that make the blues... *the blues.*

# The Instruments of the Blues

The most important blues instrument is something we're all born with: your voice!

In the earliest days of the blues, that's all there was— just someone singing in the fields or walking a dirt road. It wasn't even called "the blues" yet.

Later, other instruments joined in. But the voice has always been the soul of the blues.

Before electricity, singers had to be LOUD to be heard. No microphones. No speakers. Just raw power!

Once microphones and sound systems became common in the 1940s, singers could use more expression—going soft, loud, or anywhere in between. That's called using *dynamics*.

## Guitar

After the voice, the most common blues instrument is the guitar. But the first "guitars" weren't really guitars at all.

One of the earliest was the *Diddley Bow*—a one-string homemade instrument, often nailed to the side of a house! People used rocks or bottles to raise the string, then slid a glass bottle or knife along the string to change the pitch.

Eventually, players moved to acoustic guitars, usually with six strings. These were lightweight and didn't need electricity—but they weren't very loud.

Some switched to *resonator guitars*, which used a metal cone inside to boost the sound. Still, they weren't loud enough for big crowds.

Today, most people use electric guitars. Electric guitars were first used in the blues in the late 1930s and early 1940s. Instead of the sound vibrating from the guitar itself, it travels through a wire to a loud amplifier (amp for short) and is played through a speaker. Electric guitars are slightly less portable because of the amp, but they're loud and can be heard over big crowds.

AMPLIFIER

**ACOUSTIC GUITAR**

**RESONATOR GUITAR**

**ELECTRIC GUITAR**

### Piano

Pianos were a big part of Chicago blues and boogie-woogie sounds. The problem with pianos was that they weren't portable. They weighed hundreds of pounds!

A traveling musician couldn't easily throw a piano onto a moving train or set it up on a street corner to play for tips.

By the 1940s, most clubs had pianos, and piano blues took off. The modern digital pianos of today are much easier to move.

### Harmonica

The harmonica (or "blues harp," as blues players call it—despite rarely acting like angels!) became wildly popular in the 1940s and '50s, especially in Chicago blues.

It's small, cheap, and sounds amazing in the right hands—perfect for a blues beginner. Many great blues players got their start on harmonica, regardless of what instrument they're known for.

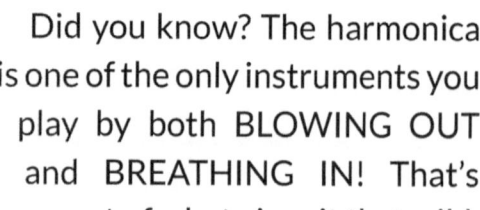

Did you know? The harmonica is one of the only instruments you play by both BLOWING OUT and BREATHING IN! That's part of what gives it that wild, bending, emotional sound the blues is famous for.

### Bass

Early blues used the washtub bass—a home-made instrument made from a big metal tub, a broomstick, and a clothesline. You played it by plucking the clothesline and moving the broom handle back and forth. This made the clothesline looser or tighter, which changed the musical notes.

By the 1940s, most bands used the upright bass (also called the double bass), which looks like a huge violin. It was first played with a bow, but blues players usually plucked the strings.

The electric bass was invented in the 1930s, around the same time as the electric guitar. But unlike the electric guitar—which replaced acoustic guitars almost immediately—the electric bass didn't catch on until the late 1950s or early 1960s.

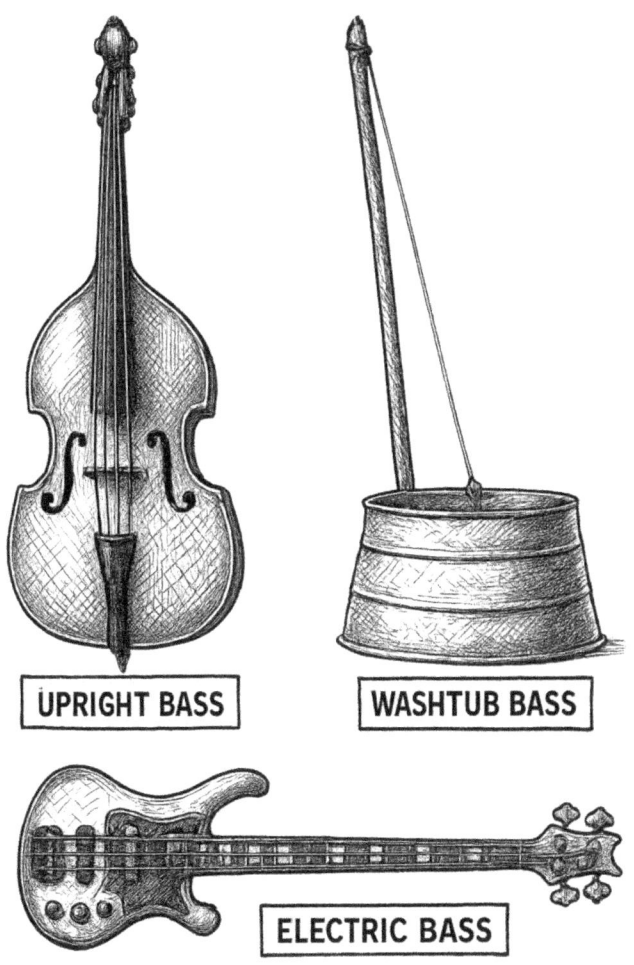

UPRIGHT BASS

WASHTUB BASS

ELECTRIC BASS

No matter what kind of bass is used, its job is to play the low notes and help keep the rhythm. The bass and drums together form the rhythm section of the band.

**Drums and Percussion**

Drums weren't common in blues until the 1940s. But percussion? That's been around forever—stomping feet, clapping hands, tapping sticks. But there's a darker history behind percussion in early blues...

During slavery, drums were often banned. Slave owners feared enslaved people used them to communicate (they were right). To stop escape attempts and coded messages, drums were banned on many plantations.

DRUM SET

Still, rhythm survived. Tapping feet, clapping hands, and shaking anything that made a sound kept the beat alive.

Even today, a blues player tapping their foot and an audience clapping along—that's percussion!

### Other Instruments

The banjo was one of the first African American instruments, brought over from West Africa. Sadly, it fell out of use because of racist minstrel shows, where white performers in blackface used banjos to mock Black culture. As a result, many Black musicians avoided it for decades. Thankfully, the banjo has found its way back into the blues.

In the 1940s and '50s, horns and reeds like saxophone, trumpet,

BANJO

trombone—even clarinet and kazoo—showed up in blues bands, especially in jump blues and early rock and roll.

## What Are Blues Songs About?

Everything!

Early blues—before it even had a name—was about faith, death, work, fear, and the pain of slavery. After the Civil War, topics shifted to poverty, injustice, travel, and unfair laws.

Later came new themes:

Trains, cars, jail time, hunger, gambling, partying, sickness, drinking, fighting, food… and especially LOVE.

Good love. Bad love. Lost love. No love.

There are more blues songs about love and relationships than every other topic *combined*.

If it's part of life, it's part of the blues.

## What Makes Blues Music "Bluesy"?

Hard to explain… but easy to FEEL.

Blues makes you move differently. You might scrunch up your face, tap your foot, sway your head.

That's your body saying: THIS IS THE BLUES!

Blues lyrics often follow an AAB pattern:

- Line A: Make a statement

- Line A again: Repeat the statement

- Line B: Say something new that rhymes with it

Here's an example:

> **A: If I had a dollar for every time I've had the blues**
>
> **A: I said, if I had a dollar for every time I've had the blues**
>
> **B: I'd go buy me a winning hand for every time I've had to lose**

This pattern repeats for three to six verses with no actual chorus or bridge. But some blues songs do use choruses and follow structures closer to rock and pop—there are no strict rules, just strong traditions.

This back-and-forth repeating of, and answering lyric lines is called *call and response*. It's one of the oldest musical traditions in the world, and it comes straight from African music. You'll hear call and response in gospel, blues, and even hip-hop today. It's a conversation—just with music!

Musically, blues also uses special note patterns called *blues scales*, which twist and bend the usual major scale to give it that raw, emotional edge.

## Nicknames of the Blues

Blues nicknames are probably as old as the blues itself. A few folks went by their actual names but most blues men and women had a nickname. While most common in the early days of the blues, nicknames are still used by many blues musicians today.

Blues nicknames can come from many things: your size, where you live, the instrument you play, and even how you play it.

Being blind or poor sighted might get you named "Blind Willie McTell," "Blind Blake," or "Blind Boy Fuller." Maybe you're not blind, but you have a saggy eye like "Sleepy John Estes" or "William Dead Eye Norris."

If you had a limp or another leg issue, you might end up with a name like "Cripple Clarence Lofton," "Sam Peg Leg Howell," or "Henry Rubber-legs Williams."

Body size and shape has helped name many blues musicians too. Just ask "Little Walter," "Big Mama Thornton," or "Big Bill Broonzy."

Birthplace or current address has helped to name many blues musicians, such as "Memphis Minnie," "Kansas Joe

McCoy," "Mississippi John Hurt," "Tampa Red," and "Louisiana Red."

The instrument you play can easily turn into a nickname too, like "Washboard Sam," "Guitar Shorty," or "Terry Harmonica Bean."

There are lots of animal names in the blues: "Super Chikan," "Howlin' Wolf," "Jimmy Duck Holmes," "Poppa Dawg," "Christone 'Kingfish' Ingram," "Rabbit Brown," "Catfish Keith," and "Hound Dog Taylor," are just a few.

Plenty of food in the blues world too: "Watermelon Slim," "Barbecue Bob," "David Honeyboy Edwards," "T-Bone Walker," and "Blind Lemon Jefferson."

A few other interesting names that don't fit the other categories are "Muddy Waters," "Leadbelly," "Furry Lewis," "Bukka White," "Pinetop Perkins," "Lightnin' Hopkins," "Magic Sam," "Lazy Lester," "Keb' Mo'," "Taj Mahal," "Peetie Wheatstraw," and "T-Model Ford."

Most of these people's nicknames have become such a big part of who they are that few people even know or remember their actual names. Try to come up with a fun blues nickname for yourself!

## But It's Really All About That Feeling!

More than anything, the blues is about EMOTION.

When you hear a blues musician play, they're sharing something deep and personal with you—and inviting you into their story.

Few other styles of music connect like that.

That's what makes the blues, *THE BLUES.*

# THE SOURCE OF THE BLUES

The blues was born of pain, survival, and strength.

It began in 1619, when the first Africans were stolen from their homes and forced into slavery in America.

The blues we know today can be about many things—good times, bad times, and everything in between. But the true roots of the blues lie in the horrors of slavery and the generations of racism that followed.

The transatlantic slave trade continued from 1619 until the 1850s. By the time slavery ended in the United States, there were over four million enslaved African people.

Slaves were treated in the worst ways imaginable. They were beaten, whipped, starved, separated from their families, and often killed. They were forced to work long, hard days with little rest and no rights. They weren't treated like human beings—they were bought, sold, and traded like objects.

*THAT* is where the blues came from.

### The Beginnings of African American Music

In Africa, music was a huge part of daily life. It was used for storytelling, celebration, spiritual connection, and community. These musical traditions weren't just for fun—they were powerful, complex, and deeply meaningful.

But when African people were forced to America, they couldn't bring their instruments—or much else—with them. So, they had to start over.

From nothing, they created something new.

As they worked in the fields, they developed new forms of music to pass the time, communicate, worship, and stay connected to each other:

- **Field hollers** – one person singing alone while working

- **Work songs** – group versions of field hollers, often using call and response, where one singer "calls" and others "respond"

- **Ring shouts** – religious rituals involving clapping, stomping, dancing in circles, shouting, and singing

Over time, they began making instruments from whatever they could find—bones, sticks, string, wood, and wire. Some slave owners even encouraged music so the enslaved people could entertain them.

But even when music was forced, it became a form of resistance. It was a way to keep a part of themselves alive. It helped them hold on to their culture, communicate in secret, and express feelings they weren't allowed to say out loud.

These early forms of African American music were the first steps that led to the blues.

### With "Freedom" Came More Troubles

In 1863, during the Civil War, President Abraham Lincoln issued the Emancipation Proclamation, which was supposed to free enslaved people in the Confederate states.

But not everyone was freed right away—slavery didn't officially end across the United States until 1865, with the passing of the 13th Amendment. Even then, slavery was still allowed in prisons.

Even after slavery ended, true freedom was still far away.

Black Americans were no longer slaves—but they still weren't treated as equals. They faced poverty, violence, and hatred. Many white people didn't want them to succeed and worked hard to keep them down.

But one thing did change: musical freedom.

Black musicians could now play what they wanted, how they wanted. They began developing their own musical styles in their own communities.

Some played on the streets. Some played in homes, churches, or parties. Some played for tips. Many played whatever people would pay to hear: spirituals, ragtime, folk songs, and the earliest forms of what would become the blues.

But even in their "freedom," they still had to deal with new challenges...

### Who Was Jim Crow?

After the Civil War, Black American MEN were legally granted the right to vote, buy land, go to school, and use public services. But many white lawmakers didn't believe they deserved those rights.

To stop Black people from gaining power, a series of racist laws were created. These were called the Jim Crow laws.

Jim Crow laws forced Black people to be separated from white people:

- Separate schools
- Separate bathrooms

- Separate restaurants

- Separate bus seats

- Separate water fountains

- Separate everything

**ROSA PARKS**

This system of separation was called segregation. And it treated Black people as if they were less than human.

If a Black person broke one of these unfair laws, they could be arrested, beaten, or worse. One famous example is Rosa Parks, who was arrested simply for sitting in the front of a bus.

## But *who* was Jim Crow?!?

He wasn't a real person. The name came from a character in a racist song called *Jump Jim Crow*, performed in minstrel shows by white actors in blackface—costumes meant to mock and insult Black people.

Even though Jim Crow was fake, the laws and hatred that carried his name were very real—and caused real pain for decades.

Jim Crow laws lasted well into the 1950s and '60s—and in many ways, their effects are still felt today.

## First Interest in Black Music

Even with so many obstacles, Black musicians kept creating—and slowly, the world began to listen.

In 1867, a book called *Slave Songs of the United States* was published. It was the first collection of African American music, with 102 spirituals and work songs.

By the 1870s, the Fisk Jubilee Singers were touring the U.S. and Europe, performing spirituals to packed audiences. They raised money, earned respect, and proved that Black music had power—and value.

FISK JUBILEE SINGERS

Then, in 1902, the Dinwiddie Colored Quartet recorded six songs with Victor Records. These were some of the first commercial recordings of Black American music—and they helped open the door for what was coming next.

The blues was almost ready to take center stage.

# THE WEIRDEST MUSIC EVER HEARD

The music that became known as the blues probably began in Mississippi in the 1890s. But here's the thing: we don't have many written records from that time. That makes it hard to know what's really true, what's been exaggerated, and what might just be a flat-out lie!

Most of what we "know" about the very beginning of the blues comes from stories that were told years later—by people with different memories, different motives, and different levels of reliability.

At one time, people said the first blues song might've been "Joe Turner," a song about a man who transported prisoners in the South during the 1890s. Others have made different claims.

The truth is, nobody knows exactly what the first blues song was. But there's very little doubt that the blues began somewhere around this time—and somewhere in the Deep South.

**Where the Southern Cross the Yellow Dog**

The first written account of the blues came from a traveling composer and bandleader named W.C. Handy. In 1902 and 1903, Handy traveled all over Mississippi, listening to and studying rural Black music.

In 1903, while waiting for a train in the tiny Delta town of Tutwiler, Mississippi, Handy dozed off on a bench at the station. He woke to the sound of a man playing guitar beside him and singing. Handy later said the man's face showed "the sadness of the ages."

**W.C. HANDY**

The man was playing guitar in a strange way—sliding a knife across the strings in his left hand, instead of pressing his fingers down to make chords. This style is now called *slide or bottleneck guitar*, and it's still common in blues and country music today.

The man was singing a song called *Goin' Where the Southern Cross the Dog.*

Strange title? It comes from a real railroad crossing in Morehead, Mississippi, where two train lines—the Southern and the Yazoo Delta (nicknamed "the Dog")—crossed paths.

W.C. Handy called the music "unforgettable" and described it as "the weirdest music I ever heard."

This might not have been the first person to play slide guitar, or the first to sing about trains, but it's the first time a blues musician was described in writing. Because he was the first to be documented playing this style of music, this moment gives us a rough point in time to call the beginning of the blues.

Because of this discovery, W.C. Handy became known as The Father of the Blues, and Tutwiler became known as The Birthplace of the Blues.

Legend or Truth?

Some people say Handy exaggerated his "discovery" in Tutwiler to make himself seem more important.

We may never know for sure—and that's part of what makes blues history so fascinating. It's filled with mystery, myth, and music.

### From Memphis to Dallas: The First Published Blues

Even though the blues had been "discovered" in 1903, it would take nearly a decade for it to be officially published and recognized as a new style of music.

Today, music gets published as recordings—on CDs, MP3s, or streaming platforms. But back then, publishing music meant printing it as sheet music, so people could play it on their own instruments.

The first two pieces of blues sheet music ever published were:

- *Dallas Blues* by Hart Wand
- *The Memphis Blues* by W.C. Handy

Both were published in 1912.

Handy went on to publish many other blues pieces and inspired others to do the same. The music he helped spread is now called classic blues, though it sounded more like ragtime or jazz than what most people think of as the blues today.

Still, it marked a huge step forward—the blues was finally on paper.

### Time to Get Crazy: First Recordings of the Blues

While rare, music by Black performers had been recorded all the way back to 1902. It was rare because, at the time, record companies didn't believe there was any commercial market for African American music—especially the blues.

That changed in 1920.

The Okeh Records label had a Black *vaudeville* singer named Mamie Smith sing on a record.

(Vaudeville was a type of variety show popular in the early 1900s, with music, dancing, comedy, and short performances. Vaudeville singers had to be entertaining, versatile, and able to hold the attention of a live crowd.)

The song had originally been meant for a white singer—but something surprising happened.

It sold.

A lot.

Even without much promotion, people bought Mamie Smith's record—and Okeh took notice. They brought her back to record again.

This time, the song was *Crazy Blues*.

They promoted it—and it exploded.

It sold over a million copies in just a few months.

Suddenly, the recording industry realized something: People wanted to hear the blues.

Other record companies rushed to catch up, recording more and more Black female blues artists.

These first recordings of Black singers launched a new category of music called *race records*—a label used at the time to describe records made by and for Black audiences.

Today, the term "race records" is considered outdated and offensive. But at the time, it was actually one of the more respectful labels used in an era when far worse terms were common.

Still, this moment marked a turning point:

Black music had finally made it onto records—and into people's homes.

With records flying off the shelves, the blues was no longer just a local sound—it was about to become a national force.

# A QUIET BEGINNING

The 1920s and '30s finally brought much-deserved attention to the blues—and to Black performers in general—but the record industry was still slow to put much time or money into their music.

### The Crazy Music Industry

The success of Mamie Smith's *Crazy Blues* showed record companies there was money to be made by having a female vaudeville performer record the blues. So, they stuck as close to that formula as possible, ignoring other styles of blues for many years. That's why the entire beginning era of blues recordings is often called the era of classic female blues.

Most of these women didn't come from the world of "down-home blues." They were trained as Vaudeville or cabaret performers—actors, dancers, and singers who did it all. These women were brought into the blues by the record labels because their singing fit this new music.

The most famous of the classic blues women was Bessie Smith. She began her recording career in 1923 and released almost 200 recordings before she died in a car accident in 1933. She was an amazing singer liked by both Black and white audiences.

BESSIE SMITH

Other professional Black musicians of the time played any music that earned them a living. They played ragtime, gospel, jazz, country, jug band music—even old work hollers and field songs—whatever it took. These early musicians were "songsters," meaning they knew lots of songs from every musical genre. This way, they could attract both Black and white audiences and earn more money.

Back then, there was no way anyone could make a living playing only the blues. Later, as the blues gained more popularity, many of these songsters began adding more and more blues to their repertoires.

### Sing Me Those "Down Home" Blues

Down-home blues, traditional blues, country blues, folk blues, Delta blues. These are terms commonly used when referring to the kind of old blues most people recognize from the movies—the image of an old bluesman at a train station, stomping his foot while playing slide guitar and singing in a deep, growling voice.

Most of the names we use today for different blues styles didn't exist back then. People just called it the blues. Some names were invented later by record companies to help market the music.

The first "superstar" solo blues player was Blind Lemon Jefferson from Texas. His records were so successful that

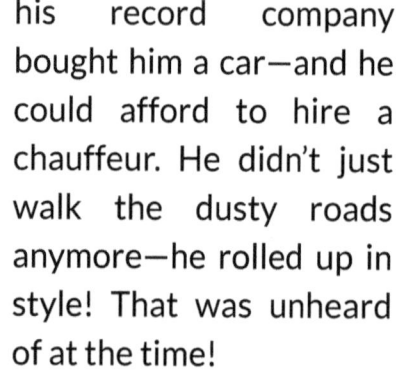

his record company bought him a car—and he could afford to hire a chauffeur. He didn't just walk the dusty roads anymore—he rolled up in style! That was unheard of at the time!

Blind Lemon Jefferson traveled with other big names who went on to shape blues history— T-Bone Walker, Leadbelly, and Blind Willie McTell. He heavily influenced their playing. Today, he's known as the Father of the Texas Blues.

As Black people started getting better jobs and had more money to spend, the market for Black music—or "race records"—grew quickly. This allowed many more blues artists to record and release music.

# The Delta Blues

Named for the region it came from, the Delta blues was—and still is—some of the most influential music ever.

The Mississippi Delta is in the northwest region of Mississippi. Full of farms, plantations, and poor people to work them—it was the perfect place for the blues to begin. It's no surprise that Tutwiler, described earlier as the birthplace of the blues, is a part of the Mississippi Delta.

The emotional intensity and raw sound of the Delta blues were rooted in the field hollers and work songs of slavery times, but now featured the guitar and sometimes other instruments.

The guitar playing of the Delta blues was emotionally intense. Musicians smacked the guitar and yanked the strings for raw, percussive effect—sometimes so hard it seemed they might snap right off! They often used a bottle or knife to slide up and down the strings, causing all kinds of crazy sounds.

The singing could range from a soft, aching moan to a loud, barking cry—each note full of feeling.

The rhythm of the Delta blues was rough and raw, with hard foot stomping giving a nice heavy beat. That rhythm didn't come from stomping feet alone—it also came from slapping the guitar strings, smacking the face of the guitar, or even vocally grunting.

The man known as the Father of the Delta Blues was Charley Patton. He began writing and performing Delta blues as early as 1910, but he didn't get any of his music recorded until 1929.

Patton was known to play the guitar behind his head, under his legs, behind his back, and on his knees. He had a loud, gravelly voice and an extremely heavy guitar playing style.

Charley's powerful singing, rhythmic guitar playing, and showmanship made him the man who truly defined the Delta blues.

DOCKERY FARMS
EST. 1895 BY
WILL DOCKERY 1865-1936
JOE RICE DOCKERY
1906-1982

Charley Patton lived, worked, and played on the Dockery Farms Plantation. The Delta blues tradition he started got passed on through many generations on that farm. Son House, Willie Brown, Tommy Johnson,

**CHARLEY PATTON**

Robert Johnson, Howlin' Wolf, and many others lived, worked, and played at Dockery Farms. In fact, almost every famous Delta blues musician we know of had a connection to Dockery Farms. Howlin' Wolf and others learned directly from Patton, going to his house to hang out every chance they got.

Of the many musicians who carried on the tradition started by Charley Patton, one of the most notable was a young man named Robert Johnson. He only recorded 29 songs before being poisoned to death at 27 years old in 1938.

**ROBERT JOHNSON**

While all the performing and recording that Robert Johnson did was in the late 1930s, the tremendous impact he had on music wouldn't begin until the 1960s—decades after his death.

There are people who say the success of Johnson's music is only because of the mystery surrounding his life and death. Other musicians of that time had long careers and gave hundreds of songs to the world. But today they aren't nearly as famous as Robert Johnson.

Part of the hype over Robert Johnson probably *is* because of his mysterious legacy. The legend of him selling his soul to the Devil at the crossroads to become a better guitar player is sure attention-grabbing! But none of that changes the fact he was a fantastic, ultra-innovative guitar player, an amazingly passionate singer, and a talented songwriter. It doesn't matter why he got so popular after his death. Many blues fans still believe he played some of the best blues ever recorded.

Johnny Shines was an old traveling buddy of Robert's, and a great blues musician himself. He said Robert could talk with you while a song played quietly in the background and later play and sing it perfectly—as if he'd been playing it all his life.

JOHNNY SHINES

While most of Robert Johnson's fame came many years after his death, he had quite an impact on musicians of his own time as well. McKinley Morganfield, a young tractor driver from the Stovall Plantation in Mississippi, was one of them.

Morganfield, better known as Muddy Waters, was born, raised, worked, and learned to play the blues in the Mississippi Delta. He was heavily influenced by Robert Johnson's music, as well as people who had been Johnson's mentors, like Son House. Muddy eventually left Mississippi and moved to Chicago, where he popularized electric blues and changed the face of the blues forever.

Muddy's story doesn't end here—we'll catch up with him again in the next chapter when we dive into the electric sounds of Chicago blues.

The impact the Delta blues had on every form of popular music to follow is huge. Whether it be rock, pop, country, funk, or even newer blues—the roots of that music can be traced back to that raw Delta sound.

## The Piedmont Blues

The Piedmont blues, like the Delta blues, started as a regional style—later reaching every corner of the country.

Piedmont blues is named for the Piedmont Plateau region of the United States. It's on the East Coast and spans nine states, including New Jersey, Pennsylvania, Delaware, Maryland, Virginia, North Carolina, South Carolina, Georgia, and Alabama. Piedmont blues is often called "East Coast blues."

The guitar playing of the Piedmont blues is closely related to the ragtime music of the late 1890s and early 1900s. Ragtime is an early style of instrumental piano music. A good guitar player using this style can make it sound like there are two or three guitars playing at the same time— when it's actually just one. This is done using a fingerpicking style, where the thumb keeps a steady rhythm on the bass strings while the fingers pluck out the melody and chords on the higher strings.

**BLIND BLAKE**

Blind Blake was one of the first guitar players to play in this ragtime style. He recorded about 80 songs in his short career, and those songs became the basis for the Piedmont style.

Piedmont blues guitar playing is often more intricate and melodic compared to the intense playing typically found in Delta blues.

Musically and lyrically, the Piedmont blues is often happier and more upbeat sounding than the Delta blues. This doesn't mean that Piedmont blues musicians didn't have hard times and sing about them— they most certainly did!

There were many great Piedmont blues musicians. Two of the most popular were Blind Boy Fuller and Blind Willie McTell.

Blind Boy Fuller of North Carolina, like Robert Johnson, died very young— at only 33 years old. But unlike Robert Johnson, Fuller left us a lot of recorded music. In his 5-year recording career, he released 120 songs.

Fuller's style was rough and hard. It combined a variety of

**BLIND BOY FULLER**

guitar techniques. He often performed with Sonny Terry, a harmonica player known for his wild, high-energy style—one of the best to ever blow into one.

**SONNY TERRY**

A Piedmont blues musician from Georgia, Blind Willie McTell stood out in many ways. First, he played a 12-string guitar instead of the standard 6-string. He also played many other instruments. He had a smooth, laid-back singing voice that was unusual at a time when musicians needed to be loud to be heard in crowds.

As with the Delta blues, the influence of the Piedmont blues is still recognizable in much of today's music.

**BLIND WILLIE McTELL**

## Other Popular Styles of Blues

There were many other varieties of blues played throughout the 1920s and '30s besides Delta and Piedmont blues. They may not have had quite the impact of the Delta or Piedmont styles, but they still played an important part in the history of the blues. Some were closely related to Delta or Piedmont styles. Others were more connected to "hillbilly," country, folk, or other old-time music.

REVEREND GARY DAVIS

Holy blues—while it sounds like a genre of its own—is simply religious lyrics sung to the tune of any blues style. Most musicians back then probably played a few religious songs, but only a few, like Reverend Gary Davis and Blind Willie Johnson, played holy blues exclusively.

Gary Davis started out as a regular blues musician until he became a minister in 1937—after which he became known as Reverend Gary Davis. His guitar playing was closest to Piedmont blues. In fact, he performed on many of Blind Boy Fuller's recordings. But Davis was a versatile musician and didn't stick to any single style. He moved to

New York City in the 1940s, and throughout the 1950s, he taught guitar to many players who would go on to become popular folk-blues artists in the 1960s.

Blind Willie Johnson was from Texas. He played religious songs in a Delta blues style. His slide guitar playing remains a huge influence on musicians today. Unlike Reverend Gary Davis, Johnson was a street preacher who played nothing but holy blues his entire life. His songs have been covered by many modern artists, including Led Zeppelin, Bob Dylan, The White Stripes, Beck, and many more.

BLIND WILLIE JOHNSON

In 1977, two records were placed aboard the Voyager spacecraft, filled with music and sounds meant to represent life on Earth. The hope was that someday aliens would find these records and learn about us humans. Blind Willie Johnson's song *Dark Was the Night, Cold Was the Ground* was included.

We haven't heard back from the aliens yet—but if they're out there, they're probably tapping their little space boots to it.

Jug band music wasn't exactly blues, but it was often blues-based. It gets its name from using a jug as an instrument. To play the jug, you "blow" into it—though it's more of a spitting action. With your mouth a few inches from the opening and your lips closed tight, you blow into the jug to create a deep bass sound. You can try it yourself with any bottle!

Even though the jug gave the style its name, it wasn't required. Jug bands used all sorts of instruments—washtub bass, tambourines, washboards, cymbals, sticks, fiddles (violins), banjos, guitars, harmonicas, kazoos, horns, drums, and just about anything else that could make a sound.

Jug band musicians were true songsters. They knew songs from all kinds of places and people. If it filled their tip hat, they'd play it! Jug band music was usually upbeat and fun—perfect for dancing and parties.

The most famous jug band was the Memphis Jug Band, from Memphis, Tennessee. They recorded nearly a hundred songs and were loved by both Black and white audiences. Their vocals were often full of beautiful harmonies.

Cannon's Jug Stompers was another great jug band. Their harmonica player, Noah Lewis, was one of the most creative players of his time.

Many Black musicians didn't fit neatly into a specific blues category. Even if they played folk music or other popular styles, they were often labeled as blues musicians anyway.

Louisiana singer-songwriter Huddie Leadbetter, better known as Leadbelly, is a perfect example. Many of his songs had a bluesy feel, but he was really more of a folk singer. His style was so unique, he almost deserves his own genre! His booming voice and use of a 12-string guitar made him a master of bluesy folk music.

LEADBELLY

Alan Lomax, who discovered and recorded many great blues musicians, found Leadbelly while he was serving one of his many prison sentences. In fact, many famous Delta blues musicians were discovered in prison. Some of them deserved to be there, but many did not. Lomax recorded several musicians from behind bars—and preserved their songs for the world to hear.

ALAN LOMAX

## Didn't White People Have the Blues?

Well, you can be sure many of them did, but there weren't any popular white musicians being marketed as blues in the 1920s and '30s. Much of the early country music had a lot of blues influence, and despite not being marketed as blues, many white country artists wrote and recorded blues songs.

Jimmie Rodgers, known as The Singing Brakeman, was a white man who grew up in Mississippi around the same time as the early Black blues musicians.

While credited as being the Father of Country Music, much of his music could be considered blues. He even influenced the playing of many Black blues musicians of the time like Howlin' Wolf, Mississippi John Hurt, and Tommy Johnson, as well as other country artists who did blues-inspired country music, like Hank Williams.

## JIMMIE RODGERS

Jimmie Rodgers, Hank Williams, and countless other country and folk musicians of the time got many of their guitar playing and singing skills from Black musicians when they were young.

One reason there weren't many white blues musicians back then is that the blues wasn't marketed toward white people. But even though white musicians weren't recording the blues back then, there were still many who loved the music and were heavily influenced by it. Over time, this showed itself more and more in the white music to come.

## Were There Any "Down Home" Blues Women?

The lifestyle of a blues musician in the 1920s and '30s was not an easy life. Hopping on freight trains and traveling to a new town every day just to play for tips, scraps of food, and a little whiskey was not something that interested many women of the time. It was a dangerous and crazy life!

There were a few women who recorded blues. And you can bet there were many who sang and played amazing blues in their homes or on their front porches. But there was only one truly famous female blues artist to represent the entire era of early traditional blues: Memphis Minnie.

Memphis Minnie was an outstanding guitar player and a powerful singer. Her feisty attitude was plenty big enough to deal with "the boys of the blues." She always played as a duo with herself on lead guitar and vocals, while her husband backed her up on rhythm guitar.

Minnie was originally from Louisiana but grew up in Mississippi, where she began playing guitar as a young child. She later ran away to Memphis, Tennessee, where she—like many other future great blues musicians—made a living playing for tips on Beale Street.

Memphis Minnie was the first female musician to travel and play that style of blues. She played and recorded a great deal of music in her career from the 1930s through the 1950s. She was so respected as a guitar player that she once entered a guitar-picking contest and beat out none other than Big Bill Broonzy—and several other top blues-men.

However, had she been born a decade earlier, Sister Rosetta Tharpe would have been right there with Memphis Minnie. A powerhouse guitarist and singer, she blended gospel, blues, and swing into something totally her own. Though she mostly played electric and came to fame in the 1940s, her fiery solos and joyful stage presence helped lay the foundation for rock-and-roll. She inspired a generation of guitarists—both blues and rock alike—and proved that women could shred just as hard as the men.

SISTER ROSETTA THARPE

## Prewar vs. Postwar vs. Modern Blues

When reading about the blues, you will often see the phrases "prewar blues," "postwar blues," and "modern blues" used to describe periods of time in blues history.

Everything in this book so far would be considered prewar blues. The war we're referring to is World War II. It began in 1939, the United States got involved in 1941, and it ended in 1945.

The break between postwar and modern blues isn't so obvious. There was no big event to set the two eras apart, although it was toward the end of the Vietnam War. The modern blues era began around 1970 and extends to today.

**PREWAR BLUES    POSTWAR BLUES    MODERN BLUES**

# AND THEN THINGS GOT LOUD!

While the 1920s and '30s built up the blues to be an accepted part of popular music, the 1940s and '50s transformed it—bringing electrified instruments, radio, urban sophistication, and the first sparks of what would become rock-and-roll.

### Rhythm Meets Blues

The 1920s and '30s saw a steady flow of Black Americans leaving the Southern states to escape the extreme racism and poverty that had plagued them for generations. These migrants hopped on trains and headed to Chicago, Detroit, and other Northern cities, as well as out West to California. There, they had a much better chance of finding good jobs.

They still faced discrimination, but in many cases, they made as much money per hour as they were making per day in the South. This movement of Black people out of the South was called the Great Migration.

The music of the Northern and Western cities was very different from the rural Southern music. Urban bands were bigger, they often featuring horn sections, and piano played a central role—especially in boogie-woogie blues. The result was a mix of jazz, swing, and blues, with an upbeat feel made for dancing.

One of the early great Chicago blues musicians was Big Bill Broonzy. His guitar playing came out of the Piedmont style, but he mixed in everything he could. He recorded solo and with small bands, helping shape the city's sound.

The sound of "Chicago blues" is a cross between the raw and passionate sound of the Southern Delta blues and the urbanized jazz blues, jump blues, swing blues, and boogie blues sounds from the Northern cities like St. Louis, MO, and New York, NY.

The Chicago blues sound was developed in the 1940s and '50s. One of the major defining instruments in Chicago blues is the harmonica, or "blues harp." The harmonica was popular in the 1920s and '30s as well, but it became a true staple of the Chicago blues.

One of the first great harmonica players was Sonny Boy Williamson. He was such a legend that a second man, Rice Miller, later began calling himself Sonny Boy Williamson II (they weren't related!). Sonny Boy II got famous playing on the radio show *King Biscuit Time* in Helena, Arkansas. The show was sponsored by King Biscuit Flour and helped launch the careers of many blues musicians.

Around 1948, the old term "race records"—that was used to

**BIG BILL BROONZY**

**SONNY BOY WILLIAMSON II**

describe records made by Black artists—began to be replaced. A radio DJ named Jerry Wexler came up with a new name: rhythm and blues. Around the same time, "hillbilly music" started being called country & western, or just country music.

## The Blues Meets Electricity

The biggest game-changer in blues history was electricity. Amplification allowed blues musicians to perform for bigger audiences and be heard over loud crowds. Before microphones and electric guitars, blues performances had to be loud and aggressive to be heard in small juke joints or on street corners.

Electrification changed everything. Singers could sing softly and use dynamics. Guitarists could play long solos.

The screaming and moaning of a harmonica played through a guitar amplifier is one of the main traits of Chicago blues. Full drum sets could finally be used without overpowering everything else.

Electric recording, which actually took over by the late 1920s, made records sound much better, too. Before microphones, all sound had to be captured through a single horn into a recording machine. Amazingly, some great records were made that way—but it was hard. With microphones and mixing boards, producers could shape the sound of a band, balance the instruments, and create a new, modern blues.

# Blues on the Airwaves

As the blues moved from front porches to recording studios, another invention helped carry it even farther: radio. In the 1920s and '30s, most stations played only country, big band, or classical music. But in the South, some began slipping in blues records—especially on shows aimed at Black listeners hungry to hear music that felt like real life.

By the 1940s, Black-run radio stations began popping up in cities like Memphis and Chicago. These small stations had big impact. DJs like Al Benson and Rufus Thomas gave local blues artists airtime and helped launch careers. WDIA in Memphis became the first radio station in America with all-Black programming—and even gave a young B.B. King his own show. Slowly, white audiences began tuning in too, drawn to the sound and soul of the blues.

Radio helped blues artists reach far beyond their neighborhoods. A song from Mississippi could now be heard in Detroit or New York. The blues wasn't just growing—it was connecting people in ways that had never been possible before.

## Chicago Rhythm Meets Mississippi Mud

In the summer of 1941, musicologists Alan Lomax and John W. Work III were traveling the country, recording blues and folk singers for the Library of Congress. While searching for Robert Johnson (who had already been dead for three years), they happened upon a tractor driver on the Stovall Plantation named Muddy Waters.

## MUDDY WATERS

Lomax and Work recorded Muddy using gear they carried around in the trunk of their car. When Muddy heard his own voice played back on record, he knew he was destined to be a pro musician. He moved to Chicago as fast as he could—and the rest is blues history.

Muddy Waters began recording professionally in 1946. He quickly reinvented his sound by electrifying the Delta blues he was already known for. By adding bass, drums, harmonica, piano, and rhythm guitar, he turned it into music you could feel in your chest and dance to. He brought the raw soul of Mississippi to the city of Chicago and reshaped the blues into something bold, electric, and unforgettable.

LITTLE WALTER

Central to Muddy's new sound was the fiery harmonica work of Little Walter Jacobs (known simply as Little Walter). He wasn't just a sideman—his inventive playing pushed the boundaries of what the harmonica could do. Walter's bold, amplified tone blended perfectly with Muddy's guitar. Along with a rotating crew of other musicians, and producer Willie Dixon, they crafted some of the most influential blues recordings of all time.

WILLIE DIXON

Muddy Waters' impact on the blues—and on rock, pop, and soul—cannot be overstated. His songs have been covered by hundreds of artists, he inspired countless musicians, and he helped define the modern blues band. He was a true gift to the world of music. The Rolling Stones—one of the most famous rock-and-roll bands ever—even named themselves after one of his songs.

**THE ROLLING STONES** named themselves after the **MUDDY WATERS SONG** *Rollin' Stone*

Other greats who followed a similar "Delta gone electric" path in Chicago included Elmore James, Howlin' Wolf, Jimmy Reed, and Sonny Boy Williamson II. While some tried to jazz up or polish the blues, it was this raw, electrified Delta sound that became the real Chicago blues.

**HOWLIN' WOLF**          **JIMMY REED**

## Serving Up T-Bone on the West Side

 Things were a little different out West—especially in California. Many Black Americans who moved there from Texas, Louisiana, or Oklahoma during World War II saw themselves as more urban, stylish, and sophisticated. They  wanted blues that matched their vibe—something smooth, jazzy, and refined.

A great piano player and singer named Charles Brown delivered just that—blues that, in his own words, was "almost jazz." But the biggest star of West Coast blues was T-Bone Walker.

T-Bone Walker wasn't interested in keeping the old rural sound. He pushed the blues toward something new. In fact, he recorded the first blues single to ever use electric guitar: *They Call It Stormy Monday (But Tuesday's Just as Bad).*

CHARLES BROWN

That song is still one of the most played and recognized blues and jazz standards today.

T-Bone's playing could be fast and jazzy, or slow and smooth—often with a "swing feel" to it. He used the electric guitar like nobody else at the time, firing off fast licks, dancing on stage, doing the splits, even playing behind his back and head!

Sure, Charley Patton had done some of that back in the 1910s, but T-Bone took it further, thanks to electric power. He didn't just play the blues—he *performed* it. His showmanship would go on to inspire future rock stars like Chuck Berry, Jimi Hendrix, and more.

# The Blues Had a Baby...

Muddy Waters once said: "The blues had a baby, and they named it rock-and-roll." As blues got louder and more electrified, rock-and-roll was bound to happen.

**THE BLUES HAD A BABY, AND THEY NAMED IT ROCK-AND--ROLL**

In the late 1940s and early '50s, artists were already starting to blend blues, boogie-woogie, swing, and gospel into something faster, louder, and more danceable. Guitar amps were cranked, drums hit harder, and piano players pounded out driving rhythms. It wasn't just a sound—it was a new kind of energy that got people on their feet.

Artists like Sister Rosetta Tharpe, Louis Jordan, Big Joe Turner, and Wynonie Harris were laying the foundation. Their music had all the heart of the blues, but with a rhythm and spirit that lit up jukeboxes and dance halls.

There's no single "first" rock-and-roll song, but several early hits shook things up. In 1947, Roy Brown's *Good Rockin' Tonight* brought a gospel shout to a blues beat. Wynonie Harris's version a year later made it even hotter.

Sister Rosetta Tharpe's 1944 recording of *Strange Things Happening Every Day* blended electric guitar with spiritual fire and hit the charts. And when Jackie Brenston & His Delta Cats (really Ike Turner's band) released *Rocket 88* in 1951, with its distorted guitar and jumping rhythm, many would later call it the first true rock-and-roll record.

In 1953, Bill Haley and His Comets released *Crazy Man, Crazy*, which became the first rock-and-roll song to chart nationally. The sound was no longer underground—rock and roll had kicked open the door. Haley later followed up with the huge rock-and-roll hits *Rock Around the Clock* and *Shake, Rattle and Roll*.

Then came Elvis Presley— the King of Rock and Roll. Like many blues musicians, Elvis grew up poor in Mississippi. Though he didn't face the racism Black musicians did, he still had struggles. After his family moved to Memphis, Elvis soaked up everything he could from the Black music scene around him.

ELVIS PRESLEY

His first hit, *That's All Right, Mama*, was a cover of a blues song by Arthur "Big Boy" Crudup. In fact, many of his early songs were blues covers.

Covering songs has always been part of music—but in Elvis's day, Black artists often didn't receive credit or payment. That was one of the biggest injustices of early rock and roll: the sound and soul of Black musicians were borrowed—or flat-out stolen—while the fame and money went elsewhere.

**ARTHUR "BIG BOY" CRUDUP**

**The Death of the Blues?**

By the end of the 1950s, rock-and-roll had taken over. It was still rooted in the blues, but now it was being packaged for young white audiences—and much of the original spirit was being left behind.

At the same time, young Black listeners were moving on too. Blues was their parents' music. They wanted something fresh—something they could call their own. That something was *soul music*.

**THE BLUES**

But not all of that youth energy went into soul music. Some of it exploded into rock-and-roll, and Chuck Berry was right at the center. With smart lyrics, unforgettable guitar licks, and a wild "duck walk" across the stage, he became one of the first Black stars to bring both Black and white fans together. At some of his concerts, they even tried to separate the crowds by race—but people tore the barriers down and danced together anyway. That's the power of music!

By the early 1960s, the blues wasn't topping the charts anymore. Many blues artists found it hard to make a living. Some shifted to soul, others leaned into rock. But the blues wasn't dead. Not even close.

It was just waiting for its next spark...

# THE BLUES EXPANDS ITS AUDIENCE

Rock-and-roll in the 1950s had pulled attention away from the blues—but by the 1960s, rock was starting to lose its edge, and young people were hungry for something more real. That hunger led them to the source—to the raw, honest sound of the blues—and a powerful rediscovery began.

### The Folk Blues Revival

Folk music and blues have a lot in common. They both use simple music to deliver a powerful message. And they can both be performed by one person with a guitar or other instrument. Many artists, such as Leadbelly, walked a fine line between folk and blues. Up-and-coming folk artists like Bob Dylan and Donovan were big fans of the blues.

Bob Dylan's folk music may not have sounded all that bluesy, but the influence was definitely there— especially in the lyrics. He even helped drive attention to Mississippi blues artist Bukka White by covering his song *Fixin' to Die Blues*. Bukka was a powerful Mississippi blues singer and slide guitarist known for his booming voice and gritty, rhythmic style.

BUKKA & BOB

Famous jazz musician Louis Armstrong once said, *"All music is folk music. I ain't never heard no horse sing a song."*

Many blues artists featured in the folk-blues revival had recorded between the 1920s and 1950s but had since disappeared. Most gave up music as a profession and returned to regular jobs. A few were discovered for the first time, even though they had been performing for years.

Mississippi John Hurt was one of the rediscovered artists from the early days of the blues. He had recorded a few songs way back in 1928, but they didn't sell well, so he returned to life as a farmer in Mississippi. Then, in the early 1960s, blues fans tracked him down and convinced him to perform again. His gentle voice, warm personality, and unique fingerpicking guitar style quickly won over new audiences. He played festivals, made new recordings, and became a favorite of the folk revival crowd.

MISSISSIPPI JOHN HURT

Skip James was another unique voice. He used unusual minor guitar tunings that gave his music an eerie sound. His performances were powerful and emotional. Though he recorded in the 1930s, he didn't receive much attention until the revival. When fans tracked him down in the 1960s, he returned to performing with the same haunting intensity—and quickly became one of the most unforgettable figures of the era.

SKIP JAMES

Son House had recorded some of the most intense blues ever in the 1930s and '40s, with raw vocals and powerful slide guitar that shook listeners to the core. Then, he disappeared from the spotlight for decades. He stopped performing entirely and took on work as a railroad porter and a cook, settling into everyday life in upstate New York. But in 1964, a few determined blues enthusiasts found him and helped bring him back to the stage. His return was electric—he still had the fire, and a whole new generation was ready to feel it. Son House became a legend all over again.

## SON HOUSE

Lightnin' Hopkins brought his gritty Texas sound to the folk revival and helped connect new audiences to the blues. His raw, rhythmic playing and laid-back storytelling style made him a favorite at festivals and college campuses across the country.

LIGHTNIN' HOPKINS

Mississippi Fred McDowell and Mance Lipscomb were two older musicians discovered for the first time during this era.

McDowell had a distinctive slide guitar style that influenced many young players, especially those interested in the raw sound of the Delta. His powerful voice and driving rhythms made his music unforgettable.

Lipscomb, a songster from Texas, was known for his deep song catalog and storytelling. He played everything from blues to folk ballads and spirituals, offering a window into the life and traditions of the rural South.

MISSISSIPPI
FRED McDOWELL

In the 1960s, folk festivals began to feature just as much blues as folk—plus older country and western acts. Most of the blues artists were older Black men in their 60s and 70s, singing about a world unfamiliar to the young white audiences. Their music became a window into a different time and place.

These musicians, once nearly forgotten, now received long-overdue recognition. Their stories and songs sparked new interest in blues history.

### Blues Research Sparks New Interest

If it hadn't been for a few blues-loving college students in the 1950s and '60s, we might not know much about the blues today!

By this time, the original blues pioneers were aging. Without timely interviews and documentation, much of their knowledge could have been lost forever.

These "revivalists" traveled through rural blues regions, tracking down musicians, conducting interviews, collecting photos, and preserving what they could. They helped reintroduce many of the blues legends from the early days of recorded music.

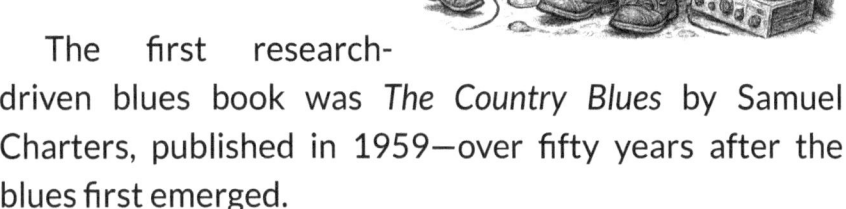

The first research-driven blues book was *The Country Blues* by Samuel Charters, published in 1959—over fifty years after the blues first emerged.

The revival also led to the release of many old recordings that had never been made public before. Back when they were first recorded, record companies didn't think they would sell—so they were left sitting on shelves, unheard for decades.

One major release was *Robert Johnson: King of the Delta Blues Singers in 1961*— twenty-three years after Johnson's death. His original 78 rpm records had been rare and hard to find. This album introduced his music to a wider world beyond 1930s Black Mississippi.

## Breaking Blues Barriers

The folk-blues revival didn't just rediscover old music—it inspired people to start making new blues again. Young musicians, hungry for something real, turned to the roots of American music.

The blues began as music by Black people, for Black people. But as the revival grew, more white audiences started listening—and many wanted to learn how to play it too. Some studied directly with living legends like Sonny Terry, Brownie McGhee, Lightnin' Hopkins, and Reverend Gary Davis. The blues was becoming a shared language, crossing racial lines.

In Chicago, the music stayed raw and rooted in tradition. Black and white musicians alike soaked it up—watching, learning, and sitting in with giants like Muddy Waters and Howlin' Wolf. These shared stages and jam sessions helped open doors that had been closed for way too long.

It was a time of big social change. In 1963, Paul Butterfield—a young white harmonica player from Chicago—started one of the first interracial blues bands. For the first time, Black and white musicians were working together in the spotlight. Times were changing.

PAUL BUTTERFIELD

### New Excitement for the Elders

The revival also brought new energy to older Black blues artists who had played for decades without recognition.

One of those bigger personalities was John Lee Hooker. Born in Mississippi and raised in Detroit, his sound was a mix of Delta blues and boogie-woogie.

## JOHN LEE HOOKER

Hooker's music had a gritty edge, a commanding voice, and an irresistible groove. His playing didn't always follow standard blues structures—he made his own. That made him tough for bands to follow, but impossible to ignore. He kept performing into the early 2000s, leaving a lasting mark on every stage he played.

### Long Live the King!

Perhaps the most famous blues musician of all time was B.B. King. He was already a well-known artist before the revival, having started recording in 1949 and scoring his first hit in 1952. But in the 1960s, he became a full-fledged superstar.

**B.B. KING**

B.B. King was so famous that even his guitar was famous! His guitar was a Gibson ES-355 named *Lucille*. Many guitar players have names for their guitars. It's often a woman's name, and there's usually a great story to go along with it... or her. Lucille was no exception.

As a young man, B.B. was playing at a dance hall in Arkansas. A huge barrel of kerosene burned in the middle of the room to keep the place warm. Two guys got into a big fight and knocked the barrel over, causing the entire place to go up in flames. B.B. ran back into the burning building to rescue his $30 guitar. The next day, he learned the two men were fighting over a woman named Lucille. He named the guitar after the woman as a reminder never to do something that stupid again!

B.B. King played thousands of concerts, appeared on TV and in movies, starred in commercials, and even has a chain of blues clubs named after him. He performed with the biggest names in blues, rock, jazz, and pop. He became a global ambassador of the blues.

Born in Mississippi and based in Memphis, Tennessee, B.B. was first known as the "Beale Street Blues Boy"—shortened to B.B. King. With his smooth singing, soulful solos, and expressive performance style, he kept the blues alive until his death in 2015. Today, there's even a museum dedicated to him in Indianola, Mississippi.

### Beale Street – Memphis, Tennessee

Beale Street in Memphis, Tennessee, has been a music hub since the late 1800s. It's gone through ups and downs—from thriving scene to rundown ghost town, and back again.

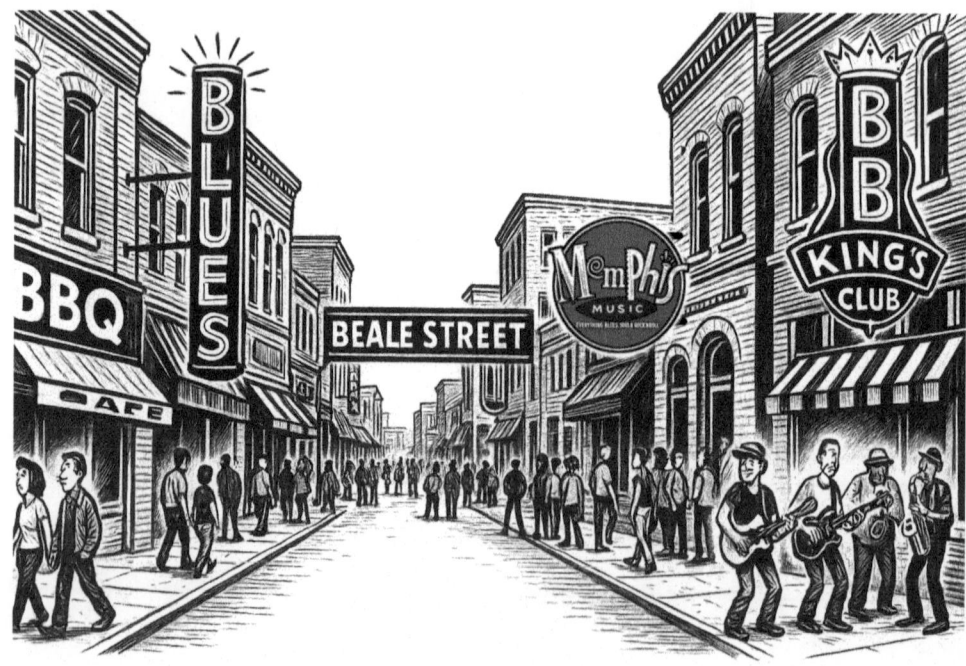

In B.B. King's youth, Beale Street was buzzing with theaters, bars, restaurants, and outdoor venues. Many well-known musicians played for tips and got their start there.

By the 1960s, it had fallen into disrepair. But in the 1980s, restoration programs brought it back to life.

Today, Beale Street is once again thriving. The main strip has five blocks of live music venues, gift shops, restaurants, and blues landmarks. There's live music every night and frequent festivals.

Furry Lewis, a well-known Beale Street musician, even swept the street for the city when he wasn't performing on it. The Memphis Jug Band and many others came from this vibrant scene.

W.C. Handy, the "Father of the Blues," lived on Beale Street. His home is now a museum, and there's a statue of him in his namesake Handy Park.

**Nearby landmarks include:**

• The Lorraine Motel, where Dr. Martin Luther King Jr. was assassinated. It's now the National Civil Rights Museum.

• Sun Records, where Howlin' Wolf, Elvis Presley, and many popular acts recorded.

## The British Blues Invasion

By the late 1950s and early '60s, blues was more popular overseas than in the U.S. While American revivalists leaned toward folk and jazz-influenced blues, British musicians were drawn to the raw power of Delta and Chicago styles. When Muddy Waters toured England in 1958, it lit a fire—his electrified sound inspired a generation and helped spark the British blues explosion.

British blues bands came in many styles. Some leaned rock-and-roll, while others stayed close to traditional blues. When they arrived in the U.S., they took over the rock and blues scenes.

The Rolling Stones began as a blues cover band in London. They're still performing more than 60 years later!

Cream brought a powerful mix of blues and psychedelic rock that wowed audiences in the late 1960s.

Led Zeppelin took Delta blues influence and turned it into something bold and heavy. Their sound helped shape American rock for decades.

The Animals brought a raw, gritty edge to British blues with hits like *House of the Rising Sun*. Their sound mixed R&B, blues, and rock, powered by Eric Burdon's soulful vocals.

John Mayall and the Bluesbreakers became a training ground for future legends, blending traditional blues with fiery electric guitar. Their music helped bridge American blues with the British rock explosion.

British blues bands had a raw energy—especially in their vocals—that helped them overshadow many young American acts at the time.

Even Jimi Hendrix had to move to England to find the kind of band he wanted. Hendrix was a Black American guitarist and singer who had played with artists like Sam Cooke and Little Richard. He formed The Jimi Hendrix Experience in London.

Though Hendrix was a rock star—one of the biggest, his playing was deeply rooted in blues. After his death, the album *Blues* was released in 1973, featuring 11 blues tracks he recorded.

He's still considered one of the greatest guitarists ever, and his bluesy style continues to influence musicians worldwide.

JIMI HENDRIX

It's strange but true: for many Americans, their first taste of the blues—a raw, Black American art form—came through white British bands.

## The New Face of American Blues

British blues and rock bands helped reignite American interest in the blues. This sparked the rise of new American blues and blues-rock acts—many with fresh faces and new sounds.

During this time, white women fronting blues bands began to gain mainstream popularity for the first time. Janis Joplin fused her raw, powerful voice with blues and rock, becoming one of the era's biggest stars.

JANIS JOPLIN

Bonnie Raitt followed with her soulful voice and masterful slide guitar. She crossed genres throughout her career, but always stayed rooted in the blues—and earned a long list of Grammy Awards along the way.

BONNIE RAITT

## Rolling Steady Through the '70s

The blues revival of the 1950s and '60s brought the blues to new heights, inspiring fans and musicians across the globe. By the 1970s, musical tastes were expanding fast—funk, soul, disco, hard rock, and prog all competed for the spotlight. But even as new styles grabbed attention, the blues kept moving forward—evolving, adapting, and quietly shaping everything around it.

Meanwhile, the legends stayed as busy and bold as ever. Muddy Waters recorded three of his most powerful albums—*Hard Again*, *I'm Ready*, and *King Bee*—surrounded by a fiery younger band and produced by blues-rock guitarist Johnny Winter, a devoted fan who knew how to capture Muddy at full strength. The sessions captured lightning—spotlighting Muddy's enduring greatness and Johnny's deep respect for the roots that shaped him.

JOHNNY WINTER

John Lee Hooker toured constantly and continued releasing gritty, grooving records with his signature stomp-and-moan style. Freddie King delivered explosive live performances and earned the nickname "The Texas Cannonball" with his raw voice and piercing guitar tone. Albert King's wide bends and attitude-filled solos influenced nearly every rock guitarist of the decade.

**BUDDY GUY**

And through it all, Buddy Guy kept the blues wild and unpredictable, tearing up stages with screaming solos and show-stopping antics. Junior Wells and Elmore James helped keep the classic Chicago sound alive, while fiery acts like Otis Rush and Magic Sam, added soul and fire to create something bold and new. Koko Taylor reigned as the "Queen of the Blues," roaring out fierce, no-nonsense Chicago blues that left no doubt the genre still had bite.

Even with the spotlight drifting to disco, punk, and hard rock, the blues kept burning—hot and steady, like a small fire waiting for just the right wind. Well, that wind was coming fast —and was about to turn that flame into a wildfire!

**KOKO TAYLOR**

# THE BLUES GOES TO HOLLYWOOD

By the early 1980s, the blues was quietly simmering in the background of popular music. But then came a blast of energy that pushed it right back into the spotlight. With a bold sound and fiery stage presence, a new wave of blues musicians brought excitement, youth, and passion to a genre many thought had grown old. A third wave had arrived—and it was loud, proud, and playing in overdrive.

### Blues Hits the Big Screen

*The Blues Brothers* began as a skit on the comedy show *Saturday Night Live* in 1978. Jake and Elwood Blues—played by comedy actors John Belushi and Dan Aykroyd—were a funny R&B duo dressed in matching black suits, hats, and dark sunglasses. They had wild adventures while trying to play their music and do good in the world. The skit became so popular that they released a real album, and it sold over two million copies!

Even though the Blues Brothers were fictional characters, they were inspired by real musicians—especially soul and blues singer Curtis Salgado, who helped introduce John Belushi to the music.

**CURTIS SALGADO**

The skit and record were such a hit that in 1980, they made a full-length movie—and it became a giant success. But the real stars of the film were the actual legendary musicians who brought the music to life. Aretha Franklin, Ray Charles, James Brown, Cab Calloway, and John Lee Hooker all appeared in the film, performing unforgettable songs that stole the show.

*The Blues Brothers* helped spark a whole new interest in the blues. And while it may have started as a comedy, the music was absolutely real—delivered by the people who had lived it.

Another movie that helped spark new interest in the blues during the 1980s was *Crossroads*. It starred Ralph Macchio—famous for *The Karate Kid*—as a young classical guitarist who discovers the blues and goes on a journey to find something deeper in the music. He's joined by actor Joe Seneca, who plays an aging bluesman named Willie Brown, based loosely on the real-life friend and travel partner of Robert Johnson. The film leaned into the haunting myths of the Delta, especially the famous story about Johnson's deal with the devil, and used that legend to hook young viewers.

While the story was fictional, *Crossroads* leaned into the real feelings, themes, and spirit of the blues tradition. It introduced a generation of kids to slide guitar, open tunings, and the emotional depth of the music. The soundtrack was packed with fiery playing by Ry Cooder and featured a dramatic guitar showdown at the end—something that became legendary among young guitar fans. It may have come from Hollywood, but the movie lit a spark that sent many future blues players digging backward to find the real thing. If you haven't seen it... you should!

## Stevie Ray Vaughan Helps
## Bring the Blues to a New Generation

When Stevie Ray Vaughan released his debut album *Texas Flood* in 1983, it lit a fire in the blues world. He brought a wild, emotional energy to his playing that blended the raw feeling of the blues with the power of rock and roll. One of Stevie's biggest inspirations was Jimi Hendrix, and you could hear that influence in both his sound and style—he even covered a few Hendrix songs.

Vaughan's music got airplay on rock radio, and he performed in giant arenas—something most blues artists had never experienced. His high-energy shows and massive popularity helped introduce the blues to a crowd that might never have discovered it otherwise. Many of those new fans followed that spark back to the blues legends who came before him. His music still inspires blues fans and guitar players around the world.

STEVIE RAY VAUGHAN

# Blues in the 1980s

With so much musical chaos in the 1980s, it's amazing the blues managed to hold its own. Disco, pop, heavy metal, hard rock, punk, thrash, funk, soul, and rock-and-roll were all battling for attention. In the past, when other genres exploded, the blues often took a backseat. But in the '80s, something shifted. A wave of fresh energy, younger artists, and a renewed appreciation for guitar-driven music helped the blues stay strong and reach a new generation.

By the time the 1980s ended, there were more people playing the blues than ever before. The blues was now shared by the old and the young, Black and white, women and men, and people from all around the world!

ROBERT CRAY

Many of the older blues musicians were still popular, such as B.B. King, Muddy Waters, and Buddy Guy. And many of the young artists from the 1960s and '70s were still going strong. Bonnie Raitt, who recorded many semi-successful albums in the 1970s, finally became a huge superstar in the 1980s. Younger Black musicians like Robert Cray gained great popularity as well.

Excitement for the blues was huge—and it only kept growing into the 1990s, where the release of music over 50 years old generated even more interest in the blues!

## The Return of Robert Johnson

Robert Johnson has been mentioned several times in this book already. He died in 1938 after recording just 29 songs—some of which weren't even released at the time. In 1961 and again in 1970, a small selection of his songs came out on LP. But in 1990, *The Complete Recordings* was released, bringing all of his known music together for the first time.

It was a two-CD set, packaged in a fancy box with a booklet full of old photos, stories, and historical info. It sold millions of copies and helped spark a wave of reissues featuring complete recordings by other blues musicians from Robert's era.

Robert Johnson's music had already inspired countless artists—long before *The Complete Recordings* ever came out. But now, a whole new generation was hearing him for the first time. Many of the most legendary blues guitarists still consider his music to be some of the most powerful and important in history.

## The 1990s – A Decade of Big Change

By the 1990s, interest in the blues had grown huge—but big record companies still weren't willing to take financial risks on blues albums. The music needed to come out somehow—so people started forming independent record labels.

Independent record labels—called "indie labels" for short—are small companies usually run by passionate music fans, not just businesspeople. While major record companies only release music they think will make big profits, indie labels helped make sure more great blues could reach the world.

Musically, the 1990s brought a wave of fresh blues sounds. With so many different styles of music around by then, genres started to blend in exciting ways. Many young players—fueled by the fire of Stevie Ray Vaughan—mixed the blues with hard rock, creating something loud and new. At the same time, many older blues legends were still alive and playing, keeping the roots strong. The result was a wild and wonderful variety of blues styles, all thriving side by side.

ALVIN "YOUNGBLOOD" HART

Another great thing that happened in the 1990s was a growing spotlight on younger Black blues musicians. Back during the folk-blues revival of the 1950s and '60s—and again during the British Blues Invasion of the '60s and '70s—most of the new artists getting record deals and media attention were white. But that didn't mean Black musicians had disappeared. It just meant the music industry wasn't looking their way.

By the mid-1990s, that started to change. More younger Black musicians began gaining recognition as they explored the roots of the blues, especially its deep connections to the Mississippi Delta. Many even brought acoustic instruments back into the spotlight after decades of mostly electric blues.

ERIC BIBB

Alvin "Youngblood" Hart, Chris Thomas King, Keb' Mo', and Eric Bibb brought the blues back down to Earth after Stevie Ray Vaughan had taken it so far out. Of the group, Keb' Mo' became the most widely known. He released several successful albums and also appeared in films, often portraying traveling Black musicians from the 1920s and '30s.

In the film *Honeydripper*, starring Danny Glover, Keb' Mo' played a mysterious character named Possum—who turned out to be the conscience of the main character. He has also portrayed Robert Johnson in documentaries, bringing authenticity and care to every role.

Chris Thomas King took on the part of Tommy Johnson (no relation to Robert) in the movie *O Brother, Where Art Thou?* starring George Clooney. It's always great when real musicians are cast in roles like these. They don't just play the part—they understand it.

It's important to understand that although anyone can play the blues, this music was created by—and still belongs to—Black Americans. The rest of us are lucky to be able to respectfully borrow it.

## Blues for the Next Millennium

What the 1980s and '90s really did for the blues was bring it into the mainstream. In the beginning, the blues was created and played almost entirely within Black communities. Over time, some rebellious white folks started getting into it too. But by the end of the 1990s, just about everyone was at least familiar with the blues.

Now part of pop culture, the blues kept growing. In the 2000s, more blues-based movies hit the screen, and some amazing documentaries were released too.

The invention of digital music, MP3s, iPods, and streaming made the blues more accessible than ever. Suddenly, people all over the world could hear blues music with just a few clicks. The internet erased musical borders, making it easy for anyone, anywhere, to discover the blues.

In 2012, President Barack Obama hosted *Red, White, and Blues* at the White House. Legendary blues performers shared the stage with rising stars—and President Obama even sang a few lines of the blues classic *Sweet Home Chicago*!

By this time, one thing was clear: the blues wasn't just surviving—it was planted deep, growing strong, and ready to inspire generations to come.

# THE MOST IMPORTANT ERA FOR THE BLUES

The most important era for the blues is TODAY! Only today's listeners can keep the blues moving forward and keep its rich history alive in the minds of young people.

The blues is everywhere—movies, magazines, books, TV shows, radio, and commercials. It's more visible and accessible than ever before.

Almost everyone who picks up a guitar—or any instrument—tries the blues at some point. New blues musicians are popping up every day, all over the world.

The blues is calling—louder than ever. If you're ready to explore it, support it, or make it your own, there have never been more ways to jump in. Let's take a look at what the modern blues world looks like.

# Local Live Music

The absolute best way to hear the blues is live and in your face! YouTube® can't capture the full power of a real live blues show. And it is POWERFUL!

A lot of blues shows happen in bars and nightclubs where you must be over 21—but if you're underage, don't worry. There are still plenty of options!

Blues bands sometimes play in:

- Local theaters

- All-ages venues

- Blues festivals (which often welcome all ages)

- Restaurants and coffee shops (especially acoustic blues)

- Farmers markets and folk festivals

You might be surprised how much great music is happening near you!

## Local Blues Societies

Blues societies are non-profit organizations that work to keep the blues alive. They're run by volunteers who love the music and do everything they can to support it.

Most blues societies:

- Host monthly meetings with live music

- Publish newsletters about upcoming shows and blues news

- Organize events, festivals, and educational programs

There are hundreds of blues societies all over the world—so there's a good chance you can find one nearby.

### The Blues Foundation

The Blues Foundation is a non-profit organization based in Memphis, Tennessee. It's like the worldwide blues society, and most local blues societies are connected to it.

The Blues Foundation does a lot, including:

- Running the Blues Hall of Fame and its museum in Memphis

- Hosting big annual blues events like The International Blues Challenge and The Blues Music Awards

- Organizing Blues in the Schools—a program where real blues musicians visit schools to teach, play, and inspire students

If you'd like your school to be part of Blues in the Schools, talk to a teacher and let them know about the Blues Foundation!

The Blues Hall of Fame celebrates people who've made a major impact on the blues. And if you ever visit the museum in Memphis, you'll see amazing exhibits about the past, present, and future of the blues.

## Blues Festivals

There are hundreds of blues festivals across the U.S. and around the world. Many feature multiple stages, food vendors, and grassy areas to relax—perfect for fans of all ages.

Blues festivals are an amazing way to explore all kinds of blues and blues-inspired music. Some of the bigger festivals feature more than 75 performers!

There are even blues festivals in the middle of the ocean! The Legendary Rhythm and Blues Cruise is a full week of live blues concerts—on a cruise ship! Musicians perform all day and night, and when they're not playing, they're just hanging out with the audience.

You do have to be 21 or older to go on the cruise, and it's not cheap—but it's definitely something to dream about for the future!

## Blues Books, Radio, and the Internet

There are hundreds of great books about the blues. Some tell the stories and history of blues legends. Others are how-to guides for learning to play.

The internet has opened up the blues like never before. With a quick search, you can find:

- Classic black-and-white video clips of Son House

- Full albums of blues legends

- Complete documentaries on the life and times of blues legends

- Brand-new music from rising blues artists

- Guitar lessons and how-to videos on YouTube®

You might even discover a young blues shredder your own age posting their first performance!

And check out vinyl records if you get the chance. Your parents or grandparents might have a record player and some old blues LPs tucked away.

Old music was recorded very differently than modern songs. Some of the magic gets lost in digital formats like CDs, MP3s, and streaming. There's something special about hearing that warm crackle of a real record—it feels like stepping back in time.

## What About the Radio?

There aren't many radio stations that play just blues.

But many stations have a weekly blues night or blues hour. Ask around or look online to see if any local stations feature blues programs.

Radio shows can surprise you—you might even discover a favorite new artist completely by accident!

## Mississippi Blues Today

What a journey we've taken! We started with W.C. Handy hearing the blues at a train station in Tutwiler, Mississippi, and followed the music as it moved through Chicago, Texas, Louisiana, New York, California, Detroit, and even all the way to England. Now we've come full circle—back to Mississippi, where it all began.

Today, the blues is still very much alive in Mississippi. From dusty crossroads to modern stages, the spirit of the Delta is everywhere. There are museums, juke joints, record stores, and festivals all dedicated to keeping that original sound going strong.

Every April, Clarksdale throws the Juke Joint Festival—a full-on celebration of food, dancing, art, and raw, powerful music. Blues fans come from all over the world just to soak it in. And the best part? The music doesn't stop when the festival ends. In Clarksdale, the blues lives on year-round.

Clarksdale is also home to Hill Country Blues—a deep, rhythmic style that gets your feet stomping and your heart thumping. And if you're into blues history, the Delta Blues Museum is a must-see stop on your journey. Since Clarksdale is just 75 miles south of Memphis, it makes for a great double-feature blues road trip.

Some of the most exciting blues artists today are based right here in Mississippi.

James "Super Chikan" Johnson brings wild energy to every show, playing handmade guitars built from gas cans and ceiling fans. He's part musician, part storyteller, part folk artist— and 100% blues. He puts on a very humorous and entertaining show.

Cedric Burnside, grandson of the legendary R.L. Burnside, is keeping the family's musical fire blazing. Jimmy "Duck" Holmes runs one of the last true juke joints in Mississippi, and plays the haunting Bentonia style of blues that's unlike anything else. Other local legends like Terry "Harmonica" Bean and are also carrying the torch.

And then there's Christone "Kingfish" Ingram—a young blues guitar hero from Clarksdale who's lighting up stages around the world. His powerful voice and incredible playing have made him one of the biggest names in blues

today. He's not just continuing the tradition—he's taking it somewhere new.

Want to see where it all happened? The Mississippi Blues Trail features nearly 200 historic markers across the country, most of them right here in Mississippi. These signs tell the stories of legendary musicians, historic venues, and moments that shaped music history—from that fateful train station in Tutwiler to the clubs of Clarksdale and beyond.

The blues may have started as local music—but today, it's a global language. And Mississippi? It still speaks it fluently.

### Today's Blues OUTSIDE of Mississippi

The blues may have started in Mississippi, but today, it's being kept alive by incredible musicians all around the world. Young artists are giving the blues a fresh twist—adding rock, soul, funk, country, and even a little punk flavor. And guess what? Some of them are people your age, or just a little older!

So, let's take a quick look at just a few of the exciting young artists who are keeping the blues alive outside of Mississippi. These musicians come from all over—but they all carry that classic blues soul deep in their bones.

Ally Venable is a young blues-rock star from Texas, with blazing guitar chops and a voice to match. She started playing guitar as a pre-teen and quickly built a loyal fan-base. Ally's high-energy perfor-mances mix modern rock swagger with old-school Texas blues tradi-tions.

Buffalo Nichols, originally from Milwaukee, is another name to watch. His music mixes old blues spirit with modern storytelling. You'll hear fingerpicking acoustic blues one moment and gritty electric tones the next. He's not afraid to talk about big topics—identity, racism, love, and hope—all with a blues twist.

Gary Clark Jr. exploded onto the scene with his mix of blues, rock, and hip hop vibes. Based in Austin, Texas, he's played with legends like B.B. King and Tom Petty, but his music sounds totally modern. His song "Bright Lights" became a breakout hit, and his albums have won multiple Grammy Awards. His blues is loud, gritty, emotional—and speaks to younger listeners in a big way.

Grace Bowers is a teenage guitar prodigy from Nashville whose funky, blues-soaked solos have gone viral on TikTok and Instagram. Her playing is full of deep groove and vintage soul, and her confidence on stage is far beyond her years. Grace is quickly rising through the ranks, performing with top artists and making waves at festivals. She's proof that the next generation of blues is already here—and ready to shred.

Jackie Venson, from Austin, brings blues and funk together with powerful vocals and a unique sound. She's classically trained on piano but switched to guitar and hasn't looked back. Her songs are full of soul, groove, and energy. She's also a tech-savvy artist who live-streams shows and connects with fans through digital

platforms—meeting young listeners right where they are.

Jontavious Willis is a young bluesman from Georgia who plays guitar, slide, banjo, and harmonica—and sings like he was born 100 years ago. He's heavily inspired by old country blues but brings the energy of someone discovering it fresh. You'll hear echoes of Blind Lemon Jefferson and Son House, but it never sounds like an imitation. It's real, heartfelt, and current.

Joanne Shaw Taylor is a guitar slinger and soulful singer from the UK who's been blowing away audiences since her teens. Discovered by Dave Stewart of the Eurythmics, she's since built a worldwide fanbase with her emotional solos, smoky vocals, and powerful songwriting. Joanne mixes blues, soul, and rock with ease, and every note she plays feels honest and hard-earned. She's one of the strongest voices in British blues today.

Marcus King is another name you need to know. He grew up in South Carolina, and by his teens, he was already playing gigs and recording albums. His voice is soulful, his guitar playing is electric, and his songs mix blues, southern rock, and old-school soul. He's one of the most emotional, intense blues players of his generation—and he's still in his twenties.

La Perra Blanco (Alba Blanco) is a fiery blues and rockabilly artist from Spain who electrifies every stage she steps on. With a vintage sound and a wild sense of style, she plays raw, high-speed guitar riffs that echo the spirit of early rock and Delta blues. Whether she's on a festival stage or tearing it up in a tiny club, her music is full of energy, fun, and fierce originality.

Selwyn Birchwood is a powerhouse blues guitarist and singer from Florida. With his gritty voice and sizzling slide guitar—often played on a lap steel—he brings funky, soulful energy to every performance. A gifted songwriter and bandleader, he's known for his originality and charisma on stage. Selwyn has toured the world, played major festivals, and proves that modern blues can be bold, thoughtful, and full of fire.

Larkin Poe, made up of sisters Rebecca and Megan Lovell, call their music "roots rock"—but the blues is right there in every song. They've taken traditional sounds and cranked up the volume with electric slide guitar, harmonies, and a punky spirit. They even do cool blues covers on

social media that get millions of views.

Tyler Bryant and the Shakedown bring the thunder with their hard-edged blues rock. Based in Nashville, their music fuses deep blues roots with big riffs, driving drums, and raw vocals. Tyler started out as a teen blues guitarist in Texas, playing with Buddy Guy before forming the Shakedown. Today, they tour worldwide and fire up crowds with a sound that's equal parts tradition and rebellion.

Samantha Fish is a powerhouse blues guitarist and singer from Kansas City. With her slick slide guitar, gritty vocals, and a rock-and-roll edge, she's turned heads all over the world. Sometimes she plays cigar box guitars or instruments with just one or two strings—just like early Delta blues players who built their own instruments. Samantha's music is blues at heart, but full of fire and energy that younger fans can really connect with.

Southern Avenue is a Memphis-based band blending blues with soul, rock, and gospel. Their lead singer, Tierinii Jackson, is a force of nature. Their music is upbeat, danceable, and powerful—and totally bluesy at the core.

Christone "Kingfish" Ingram deserves another shoutout here. Even though he's from Mississippi, he's making waves all over the globe. Kingfish's mix of tradition and innovation has brought him Grammy wins and praise from legends like Buddy Guy. Young fans see themselves in Kingfish—he's proof that the blues isn't just for old folks in smoky bars. It's for anyone, anywhere.

## The Blues Is Viral!

What's really exciting is how today's young blues musicians are using social media to reach new fans. Artists like Grace Bowers post killer videos on TikTok. Selwyn Birchwood and Kingfish drop new music on Spotify and YouTube. Festivals live-stream performances, and blues challenges go viral.

You don't need a record label anymore—you just need passion, a camera, and the blues in your soul.

Some young blues fans even learn directly from these artists through online lessons, tutorials, and live Q&A sessions. The blues is more connected than ever.

## The Future Looks Bright

The best thing about today's blues is how open it is. It's electric, acoustic, quiet, loud, raw, funky, sad, joyful—and anything in between. And it's being played by people of all backgrounds, from all over the world.

Whether you're into fingerpicked Delta-style songs, screaming slide solos, soulful vocals, or funky grooves, there's a modern blues artist out there for you.

And maybe—just maybe—that next great blues voice could be yours.

## It's All Up to You Now!

So here we are at the end of the book—but just the beginning of your blues journey.

So, what do you do now? Go listen to the blues! Tell your friends. Share your favorite artists. Learn a blues song. Learn to play an instrument. Keep the music alive.

When you discover a new blues artist, dig deeper. Who inspired *them*? Who did *they* go on to inspire? You'll be amazed how one song can lead you through a whole world of music.

You're now armed with the legends, the history, and a whole bunch of blues artists to explore.

So, what are you waiting for?

**Go find your blues. And let it find you!**

# REFERENCES & FURTHER READING

This book was inspired by a lifetime of reading, watching documentaries, and having hundreds of real-life conversations with blues legends, their friends, and their families. A lot of the information I've picked up along the way is probably even true!

These are some of the books I've read, the things I've seen, and the people I've spoken to while traveling and playing the blues myself.

## Books I've Read

Charters, Samuel B.
**The Country Blues**
Da Capo, 1975

Davis, Francis
**The History of the Blues**
Da Capo, 2003

Gioia, Ted
**Delta Blues: The Life and Times of the Mississippi Masters Who Revolutionized American Music**
W.W. Norton & Company, 2009

Gordon, Robert
**Can't Be Satisfied: The Life and Times of Muddy Waters**
Bay Back Books, 2003

Jones, LeRoi (Baraka, Amiri)
**Blues People**
Harper Perennial, 1999

Lomax, Alan
**The Land Where the Blues Began**
Pantheon, 1993

Oakley, Giles
**The Devil's Music: A History of the Blues**
Da Capo, 1997

Oliver, Paul
**The Story of the Blues**
Chilton, 1969
Northeastern, 1998

Palmer, Robert
**Deep Blues: A Musical and Cultural History of the Mississippi Delta**
Penguin, 1982

Tooze, Sandra B.
**Muddy Waters: The Mojo Man**
ECW Press, 1997

Wald, Elijah
**Escaping the Delta: Robert Johnson and the Invention of the Blues**
Amistad, 2004

Wald, Elijah
**The Blues: A Very Short Introduction**
Oxford, 2010

Wardlow, Gayle Dean
**Chasin' That Devil Music: Searching for the Blues**
Backbeat, 1998

Weissman, Dick
**Blues: The Basics**
Routledge, 2005

## Things I've Seen

**Can't You Hear the Wind Howl? The Life & Music of Robert Johnson**
Directed by Peter Meyer
Sweet Home Pictures, 1997

**Delta Rising: A Blues Documentary**
Directed by Michael Afendakis and Laura Bernieri
Outpost Studios, Tin Can Films, 2008

**Good Mornin' Blues**
Directed by Walt Lowe
MET, TCB Films, 1997

**Muddy Waters: Can't Be Satisfied**
Directed by Robert Gordon and Morgan Neville
American Masters, 2003

# People I've Spoken With

I've had so many great conversations with blues legends over the years—mostly where I just sit and listen, squeezing in a few questions when I can. A few artists I spent the most time with—and learned the most from—were Louisiana Red, Jimmy Johnson, Robert Lockwood Jr., John Lee Hooker, David "Honeyboy" Edwards, James Cotton, and R.L. Burnside. All sadly gone now.

Many of the great stories I've heard about past legends—many of whom were gone long before my time—

·MICHAEL "HAWKEYE" HERMAN·

came from Michael "Hawkeye" Herman. Hawkeye came up during the blues revival of the 1960s (or, as he humorously calls it, "the Folk Scare of the '60s"). He learned the blues directly from many of the legends in this book and was good friends with several of them. He has traveled the world telling his stories and playing his songs—and Hawkeye is still with us, still doing it! He's a great resource for the fun little stories that never make it into books.

## Music I've Listened To

Ha! Everything. And you should too! Look up everyone in this book and check them out. Pay attention to any side-bars recommending similar artists, and check them out too—even if it's not blues. It all comes together.

## About the Author

Sam Jimenez, also known as *Madman Sam*, is a lifelong blues fan, singer, multi-instrumentalist, visual artist, writer, and recording artist. He plays the blues in a "Delta meets Chicago" style, with a healthy dose of Hill Country blues mixed in. He has released several albums—both solo and with *The Muddy Sons*—and has written well over 1,000 songs in many genres, primarily blues.